ULTIMATE TEDDY
B·E·A·R

THE LITTLE BOOK OF

CELEBRITY BEARS

PAULINE COCKRILL

Introduction by Paul and Rosemary Volpp

DORLING KINDERSLEY
London • New York • Stuttgart

A DORLING KINDERSLEY BOOK

PROJECT EDITOR Polly Boyd
ART EDITOR Vicki James
MANAGING EDITOR Mary-Clare Jerram
MANAGING ART EDITOR Gill Della Casa
PRODUCTION MANAGER Eunice Paterson

FIRST PUBLISHED IN GREAT BRITAIN IN 1992
BY DORLING KINDERSLEY LIMITED,
9 HENRIETTA STREET, LONDON WC2E 8PS

A CIP catalogue record for this book is available from
the British Library

ISBN 0-7513-0002-0

Computer page make-up by The Cooling Brown Partnership, Great Britain

Text film output by The Right Type, Great Britain

Reproduced by Colourscan, Singapore

Printed in Hong Kong

❧ · Contents · ❧

❧ INTRODUCTION ❧
by Paul and Rosemary Volpp

This book is a celebration of the bears who have – over the years – given the most pleasure to the most people. You need not own one of these bears to feel a kinship to them, and to recognize them as old friends. Their influence has crossed borders, oceans, and language barriers. "Winnie the Pooh" by A.A. Milne has been translated into 20 languages, including Latin and Greek. And Pooh bear is loved in every language! He is joined by other "literary bears" such as Paddington, Rupert, and actor Peter Bull's Bully Bear.

In our collection on Buck Hill, we have three teddy bears who have reached celebrity status for three very different, varied reasons. Aloysius was famous, first, for being owned by arctophile and actor Peter Bull, who originally named him Delicatessen in recognition of his long life in an American grocery store. Then, after he appeared in the television series, "Brideshead Revisited", he

FIREMEN'S MASCOT
This rare 1906 Steiff saw active duty during the Blitz.

4

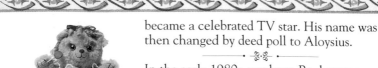

became a celebrated TV star. His name was then changed by deed poll to Aloysius.

*PERSONALITY BEAR
Created in 1983 to
honour the child star,
Shirley Temple.*

In the early 1980s, our bear, Bo, became a favourite with "Teddy Bear and Friends" magazine readers around the world. People who knew they would never own an antique teddy bear "adopted" him as their own. Bo received cards, letters, and even Christmas gifts from his friends in the bear world. Then he was invited by Jackie and Mike Brooks to attend Australia's first Doll and Teddy Convention. While there, he appeared on Australia's "Today" show, "Wide World of Sports", and the popular "The Midday Show".

One of the world's best-known bears at this point in time is our teddy, Happy Anniversary. She is famous for being the most expensive bear in the world. We bought her at an auction at Sotheby's in London for £55,000. She now spends her time making public appearances to raise money for children's hospitals. It is our wish that eventually this is what she will be remembered for.

COMMEMORATIVE BEAR
*Hermann created this bear to celebrate
German reunification. There is a small
piece of the Berlin Wall in the bag.*

❧ Bo ❧
The Ultimate Teddy Bear

Cinnamon-coloured
mohair plush.

Circular, black
boot-button eyes
set close together.

Centre seam
characteristic of
some early Steiffs.

Soft muzzle,
as wood-wool
stuffing has
disintegrated
into wood
dust.

Antique white
cotton collar with
metal stud.

Four black claws
on each paw and
foot stitched across
mohair plush.

Beige felt
pads in
near-mint
condition.

HEIGHT: 61CM (24IN).

In the teddy bear world, Bo (a 1905 Steiff) is generally regarded as the consummate teddy. Indeed, his endearing expression has driven many teddy manufacturers to strive to capture the Bo "look". He now resides in California, USA, with Happy (*see page 11*), and has made many appearances on television with his owners, Paul and Rosemary Volpp.

6

❧ CORONATION BEAR ❧
1953 Commemorative Bear

Red, white, and blue mohair plush.

Transparent glass eyes with black pupils.

Muzzle filled with wood-wool stuffing.

Head and body filled with kapok.

Cardboard swivel joints at limbs and head.

Distinctive Merrythought blanket-stitched claws.

Felt pads on base of feet.

HEIGHT: 38CM (15IN).

The coronation of Queen Elizabeth II in 1953 resulted in the production of a wealth of coronation memorabilia. Like many other manufacturers of luxury goods, the toy companies were quick to pick up on this trend. In the year of the coronation, the British firm, Merrythought Ltd., created this patriotic red, white, and blue bear for the occasion.

❧ · PIERRE · ❧
Prize-winning French Teddy Bear

Original orange glass eyes with black pupils fused on to opaque glass beneath.

Whistle added by previous owners to look like a jester's rattle.

Long muzzle with sealing wax nose.

Upturned mouth stitched with black thread.

Original beige felt ruffs around neck, cuffs, and ankles.

Unusual jester's outfit of red and yellow mohair plush tipped with black.

Very worn brown mohair plush on woven beige backing.

Large, flat feet reinforced with thick card.

Five brown, stitched claws.

HEIGHT: 36CM (14IN).

his bear won the "Best of the Show" prize at the 1st International League of Teddy Bear Clubs, held in Los Angeles, USA, in 1985. The origins of this bear, with its very unusual shape and colouring, are unknown, but his present owners suspect that he was made in France in the early 1900s. Clown bears became extremely popular c.1907–1920.

❧· GATTI ·❧
Survivor of the Titanic Disaster

Ears, set wide apart, show signs of wear.

Original metal eyes painted black.

Mouth embroidered with black stitching.

Nose hand-embroidered with horizontal stitches.

Mohair plush in good condition.

Short-pile golden mohair plush.

Fully jointed head and limbs with internal metal frame.

Short and extremely straight arms and legs.

HEIGHT: 15CM (6IN).

One of the victims of the Titanic disaster of 1912 was Gaspare Gatti, the liner's Catering Manager. Among his few possessions recovered from the ship was this tiny bear who, amazingly, came out of the disaster unscathed. A born survivor, he later narrowly escaped damage during the bombing raids over London in World War II.

❧ VIRGINIA ❧
Forerunner of the Glass Eye Trend

Long, distinctly triangular face.

Blue glass eyes with black pupils.

Body filled with wood-wool stuffing.

Nose embroidered with horizontal stitching.

Limbs slightly shorter than those of German bears.

Honey-coloured mohair plush.

Three claws stitched with black thread on each foot and paw.

Beige felt pads on feet and paws.

HEIGHT: 41CM (16IN).

This pretty little bear has no trademark (few of the early American teddy bears do), but her present owners, expert arctophiles, are convinced that she was manufactured by The Ideal Novelty & Toy Co., c.1914. As such, she is one of the first American bears to have glass eyes. Prior to 1914, the company used boot buttons, as did most manufacturers.

❧ · HAPPY · ❧
The World's Most Expensive Bear

Ears set wide apart in Steiff tradition.

Steiff button with raised lettering in left ear.

Large, brown glass eyes with black pupils.

Nose hand-embroidered with brown thread.

Dual-coloured mohair plush made specially for teddy bear industry.

Long, blunt, protruding muzzle.

Four brown claws stitched across mohair plush on each paw.

Large, beige felt pads.

HEIGHT: 61CM (24IN).

In 1989, arctophile Paul Volpp gave Happy, a 1926 Steiff, to his wife, Rosemary, as a wedding anniversary present. He paid an astounding £55,000 (US $86,350) for Happy at Sotheby's, London – a record that still holds. Her Steiff origins, rarity, size, and condition, but most of all her endearing expression, account for the very high price paid.

❧ AMERICAN GOTHIC ❧
Rustic Bears Adapted from a Painting

Imitation boot-button eyes.

Brown vertically stitched nose.

Brown cotton, polka-dot apron.

Thumb indicated on beige felt paw.

Beige mohair plush cut out from a unique pattern.

Farmer's traditional pitchfork.

Four stitched claws on each paw and foot.

HEIGHT: 48CM (19IN).

HEIGHT: 51CM (20IN).

At a teddy bear convention in 1990 in Clarion, Iowa, USA, teddy artists were asked for their interpretation of Grant Wood's famous painting "American Gothic", which depicts rural, Mid-western life in the 1930s. The winner was Barbara Conley from San Jose, California, USA, who won first prize for this charming teddy bear couple.

❧ SIR MORTIMER ❧
Celebration of a Roman Town

Large, rounded
ears set wide apart
on head.

Black, vertically
stitched nose at tip
of long, pointed
muzzle.

Safe, plastic,
lock-in eyes.

Bow tie gives
him the look of
a British
academic.

A speckled
mixture of brown,
black, and beige
synthetic plush.

Pads made
with an
orange,
velvet-like
fabric.

HEIGHT: 46CM (18IN).

Susan Rixon, of Nonsuch Soft Toys, produced this limited-edition teddy bear in 1990 to celebrate the centenary of the excavation of Silchester, a Roman town close to her home in Berkshire, England. Sir Mortimer is named after both the eminent British archaeologist, Sir Mortimer Wheeler, and the nearby village of Mortimer, in Berkshire.

❧·RUPERT BEAR·❧
World-famous Cartoon Bear

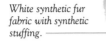

White synthetic fur fabric with synthetic stuffing.

Safe, plastic, lock-in eyes.

Black, vertical stitching on nose.

Black, embroidered, inverted Y-shaped mouth.

Traditional red knitted sweater.

Red winter coat unique to this 1986 Special Edition bear.

Yellow- and black-checked scarf and trousers usually worn by Rupert.

Soft imitation-leather shoes tied with real laces.

HEIGHT: 41CM (16IN).

Rupert Bear was originally a cartoon character, created by Mary Tourtel in 1920 for the Daily Express. He soon became a national institution in Britain, and was later to capture the hearts of many other nations around the world. It was not long before Rupert Bear memorabilia was produced, and from the 1960s, he was widely available as a soft toy.

14

❧ CHRISTIAN GABRIEL ❧
Rare, Early Steiff Bear

Distinctive seam across top of head.

Shiny black boot-button eyes.

Wood-wool-stuffed torso, head, and limbs.

Beige mohair plush worn in places.

Elephant "button in ear" (early trademark of a raised elephant).

Large sealing wax nose.

Long limbs typical of early Steiff bears.

Five black claws stitched across each beige felt paw and foot pad.

HEIGHT: 38CM (15IN).

Made by Steiff in 1903, this bear is very rare. He was made when Steiff was experimenting with teddy bear design, in particular the jointing system of their bears. Whereas earlier bears were made with a thread jointing system, Christian Gabriel has a rod that links his head and limbs. He also has a well-preserved sealing wax nose.

❧ KING ARTHUR ❧
Sotheby's Former Record-breaker

Steiff button with raised lettering in left ear.

Large, black boot-button eyes.

Nose indicated with beige stitches – a colour always used on white Steiff bears.

Torso, head, and limbs stuffed with wood-wool.

Long arms extend beyond legs.

Large, beige felt pads on paws and feet.

HEIGHT: 76CM (30IN).

King Arthur, a c.1905 Steiff bear, is prized because of his excellent condition and large size – few 76cm- (30in-) high early Steiffs survive. He broke all previous auction records for teddy bears when he was sold at Sotheby's, London, in October 1985 for £3,740 (US $5,872). Arthur is actually a white Steiff, but his fur has discoloured over the years.

❧ FRITZ ❧
German Prisoner of War's Bear

Original brown boot-button eyes.

Black, vertical stitching indicates nose.

Cap badge from the Royal Army Ordnance Corps.

Fully-jointed body, head, and limbs.

Worn and discoloured golden mohair plush.

Grey and pink hand-knitted jacket added by P.O.W..

Embroidered insignia taken from soldiers' uniform.

1939 bronze German medal (War Merit Cross, Second Class).

Woven foot pads.

HEIGHT: 28cm (11in).

At the end of World War II, this dusty bear was found under the floor of a Nissen hut that a German prisoner of war had occupied previously. On cleaning, Fritz was revealed to be a 1906 golden mohair-plush Steiff. Though his fur was discoloured and worn, he was found in a dignified state, decorated with impressive German and British badges.

❧· ALFONZO ·❧
Russian Princess's 1908 Steiff

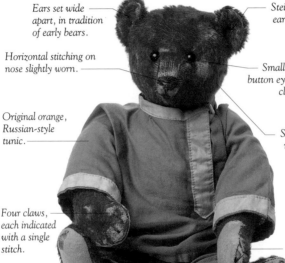

Ears set wide apart, in tradition of early bears.

Steiff "button in ear" with raised lettering.

Horizontal stitching on nose slightly worn.

Small, black boot-button eyes positioned close together.

Original orange, Russian-style tunic.

Short, rust-red mohair plush.

Four claws, each indicated with a single stitch.

Beige felt pads worn to reveal wood-wool stuffing.

HEIGHT: 33CM (13IN).

In 1908, the Grand Duke of Russia commissioned Steiff to make this unusual red bear for his daughter, Princess Xenia Georgievna. In 1914, the Princess took her bear to England, where she stayed with relatives at Buckingham Palace. She never returned to Russia. Alfonzo, the gift from the father she was never to see again, became very dear to the princess.

18

·REBECCA·

Famed as a Porcelain Plate Decoration

Covered in soft, honey-coloured mohair plush.

Large, brown glass eyes with black pupils and white ring around edge.

Shaved muzzle with black, vertically stitched nose.

Body stuffed with wood-wool – makes a crackling sound when squeezed.

Paws curve downwards – a feature of Schuco bears.

Short, stumpy arms and legs.

Beige felt pads on paws and feet.

HEIGHT: 53CM (21IN).

A 1930s Schuco Yes/No bear, Rebecca won her fame by appearing on a series of porcelain plates sold across the USA. All Yes/No bears have a head that you can nod or rotate by moving the bear's tail up and down, or from side to side. "Schuco" stands for Schreyer & Co., a German toy manufacturer that was established in 1912.

❧·RICHARD·❧
Richard Steiff Teddy Replica of an Early Prototype

Ears set
wide apart.

Replica black
boot-button eyes.

Long, jointed
arms – a
distinguishing
feature of early
Steiff bears.

White label
indicates the
model is a replica.

Design of this bear
unchanged from
1905–1951

Short-pile grey
mohair plush
only used on
a few early
prototypes.

Felt foot pads with
signature and date.

HEIGHT: 33CM (13IN).

This 1983 bear is a replica of a prototype that Richard
Steiff developed in 1905 (the original bear was placed
in the Steiff factory archives in Germany in the 1940s).
His beige felt foot pads carry the signature of Hans Otto Steiff,
great-great-nephew of Margarete Steiff, who was the original
inspiration behind this highly successful family company.

❧ ALOYSIUS ❧
Sebastian's Bear in "Brideshead Revisited"

Triangular face, a distinctive feature of early Ideal bears, has lost its shape.

Large, black boot-button eyes.

New black stitching on nose.

Scarf given by the wife of Anthony Andrews, main star of "Brideshead Revisited".

Red stitching on tongue added at a later date.

Only surviving original paw pad; others were replaced by Peter Bull.

Worn beige mohair plush patched with suede.

HEIGHT: 61CM (24IN).

For many years, Aloysius (a 1904–1905 Ideal) sat on a shelf in a New England grocery store. When his elderly owner saw Peter Bull (*see page 35*) talking about teddies on television, she decided he should inherit Aloysius. This bear won fame when he featured in the television adaptation of Evelyn Waugh's classic "Brideshead Revisited".

❧·POLITICAL BEAR·❧
Roosevelt Election Campaign Medal

Eyes suggested with tiny black beads.

Bear worn by Roosevelt's supporters on lapels.

Small, black sealing wax nose.

Low-grade white mohair plush; brown and beige plush also available.

Campaign ribbon, worn by diligent party workers.

Delicate paper paws are rare, as few have survived.

HEIGHT: 8CM (3IN).

In 1902, President "Teddy" Roosevelt went hunting in Mississippi, USA. His only chance of a kill was a bear cub his trackers tied to a tree; he refused to shoot it. Thus he became associated with bears. In 1903, "Teddy's Bear", the first American soft-toy bear, was made. This bear (*above*) was a mascot in the 1904 US Presidential Election Campaign.

❧ ANNIVERSARY BEAR ❧

Sixty Years in the Business

Large, rounded ears set on sides of head.

Pale golden mohair plush with feather finish.

Pointed, clipped muzzle.

Safe, plastic, lock-in eyes positioned next to muzzle.

Limited edition tag set in side seam.

Trademark on Union Jack label stitched to right foot pad.

Large, beige Draylon pads.

HEIGHT: 46CM (18IN).

Founded in 1930, Merrythought Ltd. is one of the oldest surviving soft-toy manufacturers in Britain. In 1990, they manufactured this limited-edition bear to celebrate their 60th anniversary. With his large ears, pointed, clipped muzzle, slightly humped back, and long, curved limbs, he resembles the models produced by Merrythought in the 1930s.

❊ PADDINGTON BEAR ❊
Well-loved Storybook Bear

Safety pin in sou'wester (prohibited in 1989 for safety reasons).

Safe, plastic nose. (American Paddington has an embroidered nose.)

Safe, amber and black plastic eyes.

Golden mod-acrylic plush.

Polyester and acrylic fibre stuffing.

Unjointed body.

Plastic Wellington boots added by Shirley Clarkson. These were later written into the stories.

DARKEST PERU
TO LONDON, ENGLAND
Via PADDINGTON Stn

HEIGHT: 51CM (20IN).

Paddington first appeared in 1958 as an illustration in the children's book, "A Bear Called Paddington", by Michael Bond. More Paddington Bear stories followed, as well as a television series, and this lovable bear shot to fame worldwide. Shirley Clarkson, of the British company, Gabrielle Designs, created this interpretation of Paddington in 1972.

❖ AUNT LUCY ❖

Paddington Bear's Aunt on a Visit from Peru

Plastic spectacles on a chain.

Safe, plastic nose.

Traditional Peruvian black bowler hat.

Woollen shawl around shoulders.

Tag pinned to shawl stating Lucy's address.

Polyester and acrylic fibre stuffing.

Long-pile grey mod-acrylic plush.

Traditional peasant-style gingham skirt.

White cotton bloomers cover legs.

HEIGHT: 51CM (20IN).

This eccentric-looking bear is Aunt Lucy who, in Michael Bond's Paddington Bear stories, looked after Paddington in deepest, darkest Peru, before his departure for England. Aunt Lucy is produced from the same materials as Paddington, but her fur is darker, and she wears a traditional Peruvian costume. She was designed by Shirley Clarkson in 1976.

❧ PRINCE OF LOVE ❧

Romantic Novelist's Bear

Eyes originally glass, now replaced with wool.

Mouth can be opened by operating lever at back of head.

Pink satin bow tied around neck.

Fully jointed body.

Paw pads were originally rexine, but repaired with velvet.

Soft stuffing, probably kapok or sub (cotton waste).

Short-pile golden mohair plush worn away in places.

Bright, colourful costume jewellery decorates Miss Cartland's bear.

HEIGHT: 41CM (16IN).

This bejewelled bear once belonged to the English novelist, Barbara Cartland. In 1988, he was donated to the Teddy Bear Museum at Stratford-upon-Avon, England, where he is displayed with Barbara Cartland's poem: I am a special teddy bear / I am very particular what I wear / My diamonds gleam like the stars above / As really I am the Prince of Love.

❖· HORATIO ·❖
The Haunted Bear

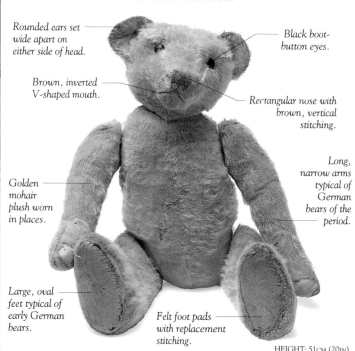

Rounded ears set wide apart on either side of head.

Black boot-button eyes.

Brown, inverted V-shaped mouth.

Rectangular nose with brown, vertical stitching.

Long, narrow arms typical of German bears of the period.

Golden mohair plush worn in places.

Large, oval feet typical of early German bears.

Felt foot pads with replacement stitching.

HEIGHT: 51CM (20IN).

ysterious tales of supernatural happenings surround this unassuming bear. Made in Germany c.1910, he was owned by sea captain, Thomas Milligan. Since his death in 1951, strange sitings have been reported: his ghost has been seen with Horatio frequently, and it's said the aroma of his tobacco fills the air in Horatio's presence.

❧ AMELIA BEARHEART ❧
The Bear that Inspired a Collection

Plastic flying goggles.

Black plastic eyes.

Body stuffed with shredded synthetic foam.

Pale blue nylon plush.

Brown imitation-leather hat.

Aviator's scarf (the bear is named after Amelia Earhart, the first woman to fly solo across the Atlantic and Pacific in 1932).

Unjointed arms and legs.

Cotton flying suit.

HEIGHT: 51CM (20IN).

This is the first teddy bought by Mrs. Rosemary Volpp. With time to kill, Rosemary wandered into a shop where Amelia, a 1979 North American Bear Co. teddy caught her eye. When recommended that she buy Amelia, the last of her kind in California, she said, "I don't collect bears". Twelve years later, she and her husband, Paul, own over 5,000!

❧ MR WHOPPIT ❧
The World's Speediest Bear

Pointed ears lined with blue felt.

Amber glass eyes with black pupils.

Motif added by Donald Campbell, who named all his vehicles "Bluebird".

Triangular nose embroidered with black stitching.

Original red felt jacket with white buttons.

Golden mohair plush worn away with age.

Body filled with kapok – a light, buoyant fabric.

Legs and feet made of blue felt match inside of ears.

HEIGHT: 23CM (9IN).

From 1956–1957, the soft-toy maker Merrythought made many Mr. Whoppits, but none led the life of this bear! He was owned by Donald Campbell, who broke various world speed records on both land and water. In 1967, he was killed on Coniston Water, England. His body was never discovered, but Mr. Whoppit was found floating on the water's surface.

❧·FIRE GUARD BEAR·❧

London Fire Brigade Mascot

Long-pile golden mohair plush in mint condition.

Centre seam on head – typical of every 7th bear on Steiff production line.

Original black boot-button eyes.

Blue woollen bib added by the London Fire Brigade.

White cotton child's outfit decorated with embroidery on waistband, cuffs, and collar.

Armband, added by the London Fire Brigade, says "bomb reconnaissance".

FIRE GUARD

BOMB RECONNAISSANCE

Original beige felt foot pads, singed by fire.

HEIGHT: 58CM (23IN)

This heroic bear served as a mascot for the London Fire Brigade during the Blitz in World War II. A rare 1906 golden mohair-plush Steiff, he is in excellent condition except for his singed feet, which resulted from his firefighting missions. He now resides with Fritz and Horatio *(see pages 17 and 27)* at the Cotswold Teddy Bear Museum *(see page 39)*.

❧· SHIRLEY TEMPLE ·❧
Teddy Artist's Personality Bear

Brown plastic eyes with black pupils.

Locks of curly hair, possibly a doll's wig.

Black thread mouth, stitched to indicate broad smile.

Baked, moulded black nose.

Body, head, and limbs filled with kapok.

Generous lace ruff around neck.

Cotton, red polka-dot dress.

Beige synthetic plush.

HEIGHT: 20CM (8IN).

Teddy bear artist, Bev Miller, designed this bear in 1983 to honour the child star, Shirley Temple, whose career in films began at the tender age of three. Known for her personality bears, Bev Miller has also made appealing limited-edition teddy bears of Laurel and Hardy, the Marx Brothers (Groucho, Chico, and Harpo), and President Roosevelt.

❖ · HAMLEYS BEAR · ❖
1988 Steiff Made Exclusively for Hamleys Toy Store

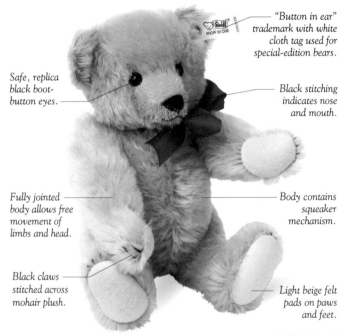

"Button in ear" trademark with white cloth tag used for special-edition bears.

Safe, replica black boot-button eyes.

Black stitching indicates nose and mouth.

Fully jointed body allows free movement of limbs and head.

Body contains squeaker mechanism.

Black claws stitched across mohair plush.

Light beige felt pads on paws and feet.

HEIGHT: 25CM (10IN).

In 1988, Hamleys, the world's oldest and largest toy store, based in London, commissioned Steiff to make a limited-edition teddy exclusively for them. Only two thousand of these bears were manufactured, each with Steiff's trademark, as well as a chest tag with Hamleys' name, logo, and limited-edition number printed on the card.

❊ BULLY BEAR ❊

Inspired by a Bear Belonging to Actor Peter Bull

Flat, rounded ears sit squarely on head.

Mohair and wool plush with cotton backing.

Extremely long, fox-like muzzle.

Safe, amber and black plastic eyes.

Long arms that curve upward at the paws.

Peter Bull's signature on label.

Large, stumpy feet with synthetic velvet, tear-shaped pads.

Woven label, bearing the House of Nisbet logo.

HEIGHT: 46CM (18IN).

One of the House of Nisbet's earlier teddy bears, Bully Bear was made in 1981, inspired by a bear belonging to actor Peter Bull. Peter Bull was largely responsible for the tremendous revival of interest in teddy bears worldwide, which ensued after the publication of his entertaining and informative "The Teddy Bear Book" in 1969.

❧ ·ROOSEVELT BEAR· ❧
Caricature of an American President

Small, black boot-button eyes set close together.

Black, rectangular, horizontally stitched nose.

Mouth opens and closes to show two small white teeth.

Red, silk bow tied around neck.

Beige felt pads worn in places to reveal wood-wool stuffing.

Three black claws on each paw and foot stitched across golden mohair plush.

HEIGHT: 46CM (18IN).

I n 1908, the Columbia Teddy Bear Manufacturing Co. made this bear, the Laughing Roosevelt, rather unkindly depicting the prominent teeth of Theodore Roosevelt. By pushing in the bear's stomach, you could open his mouth and make him laugh. Few remain in mint condition, as they have been played with, and damaged, over the years.

❖·HARMLES·❖
Boy's Kimbal Union Academy Mascot

Large, black boot-button eyes.

Worn mohair plush on muzzle.

Worn stitching on nose reveals black felt underlay.

All foot and paw pads replaced with new beige felt.

Initials of Kimbal Union Academy embroidered across chest.

Four claws stitched across mohair plush.

Long limbs in Steiff tradition.

HEIGHT: 61CM (24IN).

A large c.1905 Steiff, Harmles was the sports mascot at the Kimbal Union Academy, a boy's prep school near Dartmouth College (one of the prestigious Ivy League universities in New Hampshire, USA) before World War I. He lost his "button in ear" trademark, but all his other features indicate that he is almost certainly a Steiff teddy bear.

❧ BEAR OWNERS ❧

Dorling Kindersley would like to thank the following people, who generously lent their teddy bears for photography:

• Gyles Brandreth, Teddy Bear Museum, Stratford-upon-Avon, UK for Sir Mortimer 13, Prince of Love 26
• Gina Campbell for Mr. Whoppit 31
• Wendy and Colin Lewis, Cotswold Teddy Bear Museum, Broadway, Worcestershire, UK for Fire Guard Bear 4, 32; Berlin Wall Bear 5; Fritz 17; Horatio 27
• Donnell Library Center, New York Public Library, New York, USA for Winnie the Pooh 28
• Pam Hebbs for Richard 20
• London Toy & Model Museum, London, UK for Paddington Bear 24, Aunt Lucy 25
• Merrythought Ltd. for Anniversary Bear 23
• Sheryl Nairn for Rupert Bear 14
• Ian Pout for Coronation Bear 7, Alfonzo 18
• Judy Sparrow, The Bear Museum, Petersfield, Hampshire, UK for Hamleys Bear 34, Bully Bear 35
• Paul and Rosemary Volpp for American Gothic couple 1, 12; Christian Gabriel 2, 15; Pierre 3, 8; Shirley Temple 5, 33; Bo 6; Virginia 10; Happy 11; King Arthur 16; Rebecca 19; Aloysius 21, 39; Political Bear 22, 38; Paw Tucket 29; Amelia Bearhart 30, 41; Roosevelt Bear 36; Harmles 37
• Ankie Wild, Ribchester Museum of Childhood, Ribchester, Lancashire, UK for Gatti 9

Thanks also to Barbara Cartland, whose bear, Prince of Love, is on loan to the Teddy Bear Museum, Stratford-upon-Avon, UK.

❖ USEFUL ADDRESSES ❖

The Bear Museum
Judy Sparrow
38 Dragon Street
Petersfield
Hampshire GU31 4JJ
☎ 0730 65108

Bethnal Green Museum of Childhood
Cambridge Heath Road
London E2 9PA
☎ 081 981 1711/6789

The London Toy and Model Museum
21/23 Craven Hill
London W2 3EN
☎ 071 262 9450/7905

Cotswold Teddy Bear Museum
76 High Street
Broadway
Worcestershire WR12 7AJ
☎ 0386 858323

Merrythought's Shop and Museum
Dale End, Ironbridge
Telford
Shropshire TF8 7NJ
☎ 0952 433029

The Teddy Bear Museum
19 Greenhill Street
Stratford-upon-Avon
Warwickshire CV37 6LF
☎ 0789 293160

·❧· INDEX ·❧·

·ACKNOWLEDGMENTS·

Dorling Kindersley would like to thank the following photographers for their contributions to this book: Jim Coit 1, 2, 3, 5 (top), 6, 8, 10, 11, 12, 15, 16, 19, 21, 22, 29, 30, 33, 36, 37, 38, 39, 41; Peter Anderson 4, 5, 17, 27, 32; Roland Kemp 7, 13, 14, 18, 20, 23, 24, 25, 26, 34; Lynton Gardiner 28; Matthew Ward 9, 31, 35.

We would also like to thank the following for their help: Laaren Brown and Susan Thompson for editorial help; Pauline Bayne, Ann Terrell, and Sam Grimmer for design assistance; Alastair Wardle and Peter Howlett for their DTP expertise; and Michael Allaby for the index. Our special thanks go to Paul and Rosemary Volpp for their patience and generous contributions to the book.

The author would like to thank Jane Domican and the sales staff of the soft toy department at Hamleys, London; Oliver Holmes and John Parkes at Merrythought Ltd.; Susan Rixon at Nonsuch Soft Toys; Shirley Clarkson of Gabrielle Designs; Jack Wilson; and Sylvia Cootes and staff at the Teddy Bear Museum, Stratford-upon-Avon, UK.

Border illustrations by Pauline Bayne.
Illustrated letters by Gillie Newman.